ULTIMATE TEDDY BEAR JOURNAL

THIS BOOK BELONGS TO

....